I AM...
BiGGER

And So Are You

JAX LAKE

Dedicated to my brilliant, compassionate, funny,
talented, loving and amazing children,

Xavier & Olivia
XOXO

Skills For The Soul

BE KIND. **LOVE WITHOUT CONDITIONS.** BE RESPONSIBLE. YOU ARE WORTHY. BE BRAVE. TAKE RISKS. BE CONSIDERATE. GO HARD. BREATHE SLOWLY. **NEVER SETTLE.** **YOU ARE POWERFUL.** YOU HAVE THE RIGHT TO SAY NO. BE RESILIENT. LIVE FEARLESSLY. **ENGAGE.** HELP OTHERS. VALUE YOU. BE BOLD. **MAKE WISE DECISIONS.** USE YOUR INTELLECT OVER YOUR EMOTIONS. STAY READY SO YOU DON'T HAVE TO GET READY. **THINK GLOBALLY.** LOVE OTHERS. **BE OTIMISTIC.** THINK OUT OF THE BOX. ALWAYS HAVE OPEN ARMS. BE THE BEST YOU COULD BE. ALWAYS BE AWARE OF YOUR SURROUNDINGS. **BE MINDFUL** OF THE COMPANY YOU KEEP. DON'T TAKE NO FOR AN ANSWER. IN SOME BATTLES YOU JUST HAVE TO BACK DOWN. YOU DON'T LOSE YOU **LEARN.** LIVE ANOTHER DAY. **YOU ARE BIGGER.** YOUR START DOES NOT DETERMINE YOUR FINISH. LET GO. BREATHE. LOOK UP. DANCE. SHOW THANKS. BE HONEST. **NOURISH YOUR SOUL.** BE KIND. LOVE WITHOUT CONDITIONS. TRUST YOUR INSTINCTS. **KNOW GOD.** TRUST. BE BRAVE. **TAKE RISKS.** BE CONSIDERATE. GO HARD. NEVER SETTLE. KNOW YOUR WORTH. LAUGH. BE YOU. IT'S OKAY TO CRY. BE PATIENT. BE CONSISTENT. **PASSION.** EQUALITY. HAVE CONFIDENCE. **FORGIVE** AND BE FREE. VALUE YOU. **BE BOLD.** SMILE. MAKE WISE DECISIONS. BE COMPETENT. SHOW THANKS. GIVE. YOU ARE A PRODUCT OF YOUR **CHOICES.** BELIEVE. **FEAR LESS.** TAKE A RISK. LOVE. MUSIC. INTELLECT OVER EMOTIONS. BE OPTIMISTIC. HAVE PATIENCE. THINK OUT OF THE BOX. **ALWAYS HAVE AN OPEN MIND.** BE THE BEST YOU CAN BE. ALWAYS BE AWARE OF YOUR SURROUNDINGS. BE MINDFUL OF THE COMPANY YOU KEEP. **SEEK PEACE.** LISTEN. DON'T TAKE NO FOR AN ANSWER. YOU DON'T LOSE YOU LEARN. **IT IS OKAY TO CRY.** LIVE.

I have a VISION
and hills of GOALS
My PURPOSE
Lies deep down
within my
SOUL.

VISION
PLAN
ACTION
SUCCESS

I am special and so are you.
Don't ever let anyone tell you differently
Because that is not true.

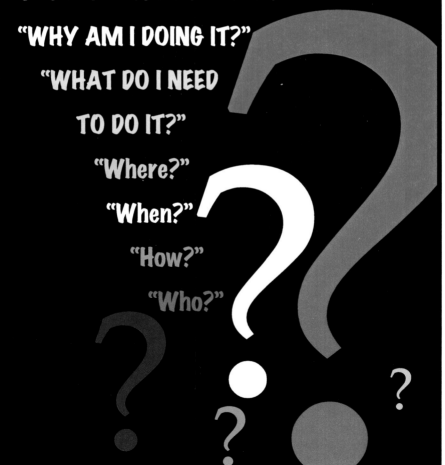

Take the time to look within
and honestly ask yourself...

"HOW AM I DOING?"

"WHAT AM I DOING?"

"WHY AM I DOING IT?"

"WHAT DO I NEED

TO DO IT?"

"Where?"

"When?"

"How?"

"Who?"

SELF-REFLECTION AND

EXAMINE YOUR CHARACTER, ACTIONS & INTENTIONS.

INTROSPECTION

EXPLORE YOUR MENTAL AND EMOTIONAL STATE OF MIND & WELL BEING.

Can lead you to have a

HEALTHY SELF-PERCEPTION

YOUR ATTITUDES AND PREFERENCES ARE A RESPONSE TO THE WAY YOU SEE & FEEL ABOUT YOURSELF. FEEL GOOD ABOUT WHO YOU ARE.

WHAT DO I WANT? WHAT DO I NEED?

HOW CAN I HELP OTHERS IF I DON'T UNDERSTAND ME?

GET TO KNOW YOU. LEARN TO LIVE WITHOUT AN ABUNDANCE OF WORRY, FEAR & DOUBT. ALWAYS BELIEVE IN YOURSELF.

Change your thoughts and your feelings will change too.

Think about the results
And your actions will change...
'Tis true!

Set your sights on mountaintops.
Keep on striving and

NEVER

STOP

Through the valley
And up again,
Keep on pushing
Until you win!

Giving up
is not an option.
Keep on climbing and
don't think about stopping.

A loss is simply
A chance to learn.

Seek knowledge and
continue to yearn.

HAVE A POWERFUL DESIRE
TO EVOLVE, LEARN & GROW

Sometimes I feel

FRUSTRATED

When I look around.

So I make it MY DUTY to
CHANGE THE SOUND.

The words, the images,
The sights I see...

I WILL NOT
LET NEGATIVITY
DEFINE OR CHANGE ME!

Life may not be easy.
Life may not seem fair.

Use your
Intellect over your Emotions

and a solution will always be there.

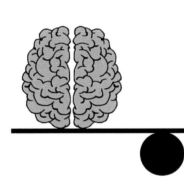

Think first...

It just makes sense.
It will save you heartache, time and
perhaps a few dollars and cents.

Remain positive & focused
And ignore all of the
Hubbub & Hokus Pokus.

UPROAR, NONSENSE, DRAMA & TRICKERY

Some people are MEAN.
Some people are actually
quite RUDE.

Simply remind them,
"DUDE...THAT'S SO NOT COOL!"

Stand up for something
Or you will fall for anything.

Stand strong
When you see wrong.

Treat Others
How you would like for them to treat you.

Make people smile
Not sad and blue.

Do what is right
Whether day or night.
Alone or with a friend,
Be true to you and trust your
INTUITION.

INTUITION: THE CORE OF YOUR INTERNAL COMPASS THAT GUIDES YOUR DECISION-MAKING (CHOICES) WITHOUT CONSCIOUS REASONING (THINKING ABOUT IT); YOUR HEART AND YOUR MIND.

14

NEVER UNDERESTIMATE
The POWER of your WORDS.

Use them to

SPEAK

LiFE

NOT

PAIN, DESTRUCTION AND HURT.

Make GOOD CHOICES...

DON'T DO DRUGS

So your DREAMS don't get SWEPT UNDER THE RUG.

Self-Respect
Family

Drugs will make you feel

ICKY and SICK

 All over

So make sure you ALWAYS
REMAIN CLEAN AND SOBER!

FREE OF MIND ALTERING SUBSTANCES

It only takes one time to get you hooked. So
don't even try it because it is not a good look.

16

BE A LEADER

SET THE PACE.
Life is a marathon,
<u>Not</u> a quick and easy race.

LEAD WITH INTEGRITY

GOOD CHARACTER

LEAD WITH PRECISION

EXACTNESS

LEAD WITHOUT FEAR,
RATHER AMBITION & INTENTION

HARD WORK, DETERMINATION & A PLAN

NEVER FORGET
YOUR GOALS AND NEVER EVER
LOSE SITE OF YOUR VISION.

WHAT YOU WANT TO ACCOMPLISH

Brush your teeth three times a day. Listen to your doctor to keep the cooties away.

Eat **HEALTHY FOODS** and **EXERCISE** too. It will promote healthy living and **longevity** too.

A LONG LIFE

Get plenty of **REST** &

PLEASE DON'T STRESS...

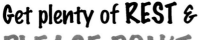

Keep your life **BALANCED** and be your absolute **BEST.**

Read

Lots of books and

Challenge

Your mind

Go on a

MENTAL JOURNEY;

It is so

DIVINE.

Make sure you respect

MONEY,

And pay your bills on time.
Be a responsible spender,
Not wasteful all the time.
Invest and save your money,
it can grow while you sleep.
Make wise decisions and more
money you will meet. reap. keep.

Invest. Save.
Travel. Have
Fun. Help
Others.

CHA-CHING!

BUY A HOUSE

Maybe one or two...What the heck buy a few.
Don't stop there...Buy the block,
buy the town...buy a whole lot!

With a great R.O.I.,
you can go anywhere in the world
you want to fly.....*Zoooommmmmm*

Adiós, Au revoir, Tschüss, Bye Bye...

ROI (Return on Investment) | The money you earn from your investment.

"Bye Bye"
Adiós, Au revoir, Tschüss
Spanish, French & German

22

Start a business.
Take a risk.

You'll never
know what you
can do if you don't
go for it!

Fear less.
Believe more.
Trust yourself
from your core.

ALWAYS BE ON TIME & DON'T DO CRIME
DON'T STEAL. DON'T CHEAT. DON'T LIE.

And know...
That it's okay to sometimes cry.

Crying can cleanse your soul
And help you refocus to achieve your goals.

HAVE A PASSION,
MAKE A PLAN,
TAKE A LEAP...

SET YOUR SIGHTS HIGH AND

WORK REAL HARD

HAVE FAITH AND YOU

WILL GO **FARRRRRRRRR...**

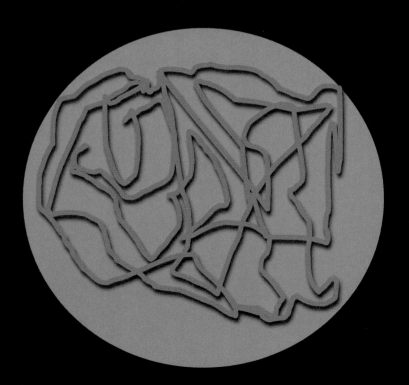

YOU CAN BE
WHATEVER YOU WANT TO BE.
EDUCATE YOURSELF
AND IT WILL SET YOU FREE.

MOST IMPORTANTLY...
NEVER EVER BE A

Bullies are in pain and their goal
is to crush your spirit and
make you feel the same.

You never know from which people come...
So have a lil' Tolerance, Compassion,
Patience, Love & Respect
for everyone.

YOU

ARE

BiGGER

YOU ARE AS BIG AS CAN BE

Your circumstances
Don't determine
Who you will
One day be.

Bloom where you are planted
and never take life for granted.

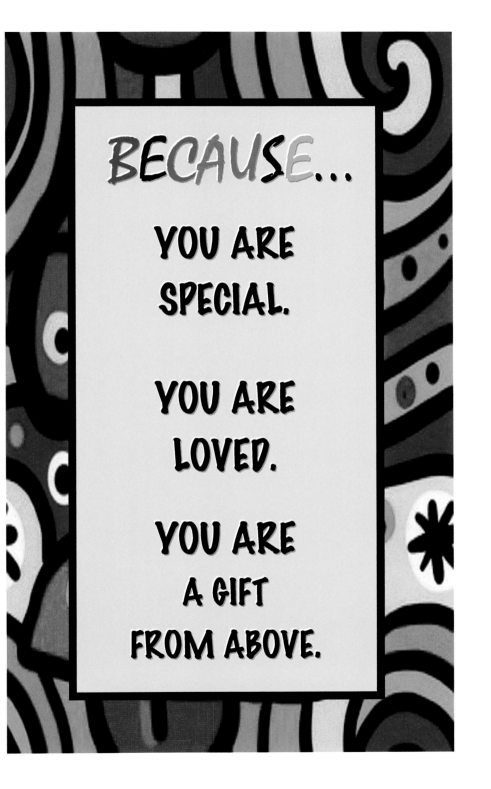

NOW SPREAD YOUR WINGS & SOAR REAL HIGH.

BE A GLOBAL LEADER & HELP OTHERS LEARN TO FLY

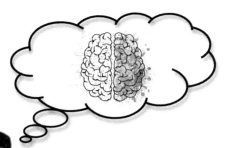

Always make sure to
USE YOUR BRAIN
And
BE PROUD
of your
GIVEN NAME.

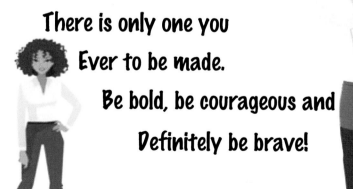

There is only one you
Ever to be made.
Be bold, be courageous and
Definitely be brave!

Be KIND
And let your
LIGHT SO SHINE.
KNOW YOUR VALUE.
KNOW YOUR WORTH.

KNOW THAT NO ONE HAS THE RIGHT TO
TOUCH YOU INAPPROPRIATELY OR
MAKE YOU HURT.

STAND UP TALL
& NEVER PLAY SMALL!

A HERO YOU ARE

A HERO INDEED

Never forget your manners

SMILE

"Hello"
"Thank You" and "Please"

BONSWA	**NAMASTE**	**BONJOUR**	**NDE-EWO**	**KONNICHIWA**
(HELLO)	(HELLO)	(HELLO)	(HELLO)	(HELLO)
Creole	Hindi	French	Igbo	Japanese

SALAMAT	**SHUKRAN**	**DO JEH**	**GRAZIE**	**ARIGATO**
(THANK YOU)	(THANK YOU)	(THANK YOU)	(THANK YOU)	(THANK YOU)
Tagalog	Arabic	Cantonese	Italian	Japanese

HOLA	**GUTEN TAG**	**TACK**	**TAFADHALI**	**JABULISA**	**EFHARISTO**
(HELLO)	(HELLO)	(PLEASE)	(PLEASE)	(PLEASE)	(THANK YOU)
Spanish	German	Swedish	Swahili	Zulu	Greek

I AM BiGGER

I AM AS BiG AS CAN BE.

I WILL BECOME SUCCESSFUL
AND BECOME WHATEVER
I WORK HARD TO BE!

**I AM BiGGER
AND SO ARE
YOU.**

**NOW LET'S DO
WHAT WE'VE
GOT TO DO!**

The Beginning

There are
no such things as endings...
Just the beginning of a new chapter.

Practice these principles And they will set you free!

BE KIND. LOVE WITHOUT CONDITIONS. BE RESPONSIBLE. YOU ARE WORTHY. **BE BRAVE.** TAKE RISKS. BE CONSIDERATE. **GO HARD.** BREATHE SLOWLY. NEVER SETTLE. YOU ARE POWERFUL. **YOU HAVE THE RIGHT TO SAY NO**. **BE RESILIENT.** LIVE FEARLESSLY. ENGAGE. HELP OTHERS. **VALUE YOU.** BE BOLD. **MAKE WISE DECISIONS.** USE YOUR INTELLECT OVER YOUR EMOTIONS. **STAY READY** SO YOU DON'T HAVE TO GET READY. THINK GLOBALLY. LOVE OTHERS. **BE OTIMISTIC.** THINK OUT OF THE BOX. ALWAYS HAVE OPEN ARMS. BE THE BEST YOU COULD BE. ALWAYS BE AWARE OF YOUR SURROUNDINGS. **BE MINDFUL** OF THE COMPANY YOU KEEP. DON'T TAKE NO FOR AN ANSWER. **IN SOME BATTLES YOU JUST HAVE TO BACK DOWN.** YOU DON'T LOSE YOU LEARN. **LIVE ANOTHER DAY.** YOU ARE BIGGER. YOUR START DOES NOT DETERMINE YOUR FINISH. **LET GO.** BREATHE. LOOK UP. **DANCE.** SHOW THANKS. **BE HONEST.** NOURISH YOUR SOUL. BE KIND. LOVE WITHOUT CONDITIONS. **TRUST YOUR INSTINCTS.** KNOW GOD. TRUST. BE BRAVE. TAKE RISKS. **BE CONSIDERATE.** GO HARD. NEVER SETTLE. **KNOW YOUR WORTH**. LAUGH. BE YOU. IT'S OKAY TO CRY. BE PATIENT. **BE CONSISTENT.** PASSION. **EQUALITY.** HAVE CONFIDENCE. FORGIVE AND BE FREE. VALUE YOU. BE BOLD. **SMILE.** MAKE WISE DECISIONS. **BE COMPETENT**. SHOW THANKS. GIVE. YOU ARE A PRODUCT OF YOUR CHOICES. **BELIEVE.** FEAR LESS. **TAKE A RISK. LOVE. MUSIC. INTELLECT OVER EMOTIONS.** BE OPTIMISTIC. HAVE PATIENCE. **USE YOUR VOICE.** HAVE AN OPEN MIND. BE THE BEST YOU CAN BE. **ALWAYS BE AWARE OF YOUR SURROUNDINGS. SEEK PEACE. LISTEN. RESPECT.**

Do all things with Love

I am Bigger and So are You!

JACQUELYN "JAX" LAKE, MHS

is an Author, Global Speaker, Celebrity & Pro Sports Life Strategist, Social Entrepreneur, Educator, Recovery Coach, Thought Leader, Parenting Expert and Founder of a Non-profit (The Altruism Initiative) through which she strengthens children and families through Global Leadership, Social Innovation and Empowerment via Education, Sports and the Arts.

"We all possess the capacity to change. Yet, we must first ignite the desire."

— Jax Lake

www.jaxlake.com
IAmJaxLake@gmail.com
Instagram:
@IAmJaxLake
@SkillsForTheSoul

MORRISTOWN, NJ | NEWARK, NJ

Made in the USA
Middletown, DE
11 September 2020